in
the
news™

DARFUR

AFRICAN GENOCIDE

John Xavier

ROSEN
PUBLISHING®

New York

To the people of Darfur

Published in 2008 by The Rosen Publishing Group, Inc.
29 East 21st Street, New York, NY 10010

First Edition

Library of Congress Cataloging-in-Publication Data

Xavier, John.
Darfur: African genocide / John Xavier. — 1st ed.
  p. cm. — (In the news)
Includes bibliographical references and index.
ISBN-13: 978-1-4042-1912-0
ISBN-10: 1-4042-1912-9
1. Sudan—History—Darfur conflict, 2003– 2. Ethnic conflict—Sudan—Darfur. 3. Genocide—Sudan—Darfur. 4. Crimes against humanity—Sudan—Darfur region. I. Title.
DT159.6.D27X38 2008
962.404'3—dc22

2007002909

Manufactured in the United States of America

On the cover: *(Clockwise from top right)* A Sudanese rebel fighter watches helplessly as a village burns less than an hour after a janjaweed attack. A refugee from Darfur with her daughter carries firewood across the desert terrain in Chad. Many displaced people from Darfur have sought refuge in Chad. Sudan Liberation Army (SLA) rebels patrol northern Darfur against attacks by the Sudanese army.

contents

An Overview of the Crisis in Darfur

Darfur is the western region of the African country of Sudan. In recent years, the people of Darfur have been systematically attacked by the Sudanese army and by proxy-militia controlled by the Sudanese government. These militia bands are called the janjaweed. Some believe that "janjaweed" is a combination of the Arabic words *jinn* (spirit) and *jawad* (horse). It also has been interpreted as a combination of the words for evil and horse, translated as "devils on horseback." Another theory traces the word's origins to the Persian language, Farsi. According to this explanation, "janjaweed" is derived from the Persian word for war (*jang*) and "janjaweed" means "warrior."

Darfur contains some of the most remote geography in the world. Much of the region is not accessible by roads. Most of the six million inhabitants live in small towns and rely on farming or herding for their survival. Yet despite its outward appearance, Darfur has a rich culture with vast ethnic diversity and an intricate, ancient system of resolving conflict. It also has great political significance in Sudan's government. These factors make the conflict both important and complex.

The escalating violence in Darfur has resulted in an estimated 200,000 to 500,000 deaths since 2003. In other words, approximately one in twelve people have been killed from 2003 to 2006. Attacks on villages take the form of raids, where the janjaweed arrive on horses, camels, or in automobiles. They pillage the villages, stealing anything of value. The villagers are often raped and tortured, and many are murdered. These attacks are followed by aerial assault from the Sudanese military. Planes bomb the villages, and then the Sudanese soldiers attack on foot, killing and raping more villagers. Finally, the soldiers burn what is not already destroyed. The villages are left decimated so that no survivors can return.

The soldiers and the janjaweed use rape as a means of warfare, and countless females of all ages have been assaulted in this way. It is estimated that more than 2,000 villages have been destroyed. Villagers who are not killed are suddenly homeless; the number of homeless has been estimated at more than two million. Many of these refugees have sought asylum in refugee camps in the neighboring country of Chad.

In order to understand the cause of this conflict, it is important to realize that Sudan has been in an almost constant state of civil war since it gained independence

A Sudanese woman and her baby sit with the remains of their home in the village of Juba, Sudan. It was set on fire during a Sudan People's Liberation Army (SPLA) counterattack.

from Great Britain in 1956. Two civil wars have followed, as have periods of severe drought that resulted in deadly famines. The first civil war ended in 1972; the second began in 1983. (The civil war and the preceding famine left an estimated two million dead and four million homeless.)

North vs. South

There are three major parties in these affairs: the North (the official Sudanese government); the South (antigovernment rebel groups); and Darfur, which is the western region of Sudan.

The civil wars have been between the North and the South. The people of the North are primarily Arab Muslims and are the ruling government, headquartered in the capital city of Khartoum. The people of the South are primarily non-Muslims. Some of them are African Christians; many are animists, or pagans (although the word "pagan" is considered insulting and is not generally used). The vast majority of the population of Sudan is Sunni Muslim. (Sunni and Shiite are the two major branches of Islam.) Overall, approximately 70 percent of Sudanese are Muslim, while only about 5 percent is Christian. The remaining 25 percent of the population is animist.

The current leader of Sudan, General Omar Hassan al-Bashir, gained power in 1989 as the result of a military coup in Khartoum. When al-Bashir took control, certain Islamic laws were adopted as the basis of the government. This pressing of Sudan toward fundamentalist Islam was one of several reasons that many of the African tribes in the South began to resist the government.

The conflict between the government and the rebel groups was also due to other factors, including land rights, a demand for infrastructure, the availability of weapons from other countries, economic survival, drought, famine, and disease. Over the past two decades, major resistance groups have developed in opposition to al-Bashir's regime. In southern Sudan, the Sudan People's Liberation Army (SPLA), comprised of African Christians, started a revolt—known as an insurgency—against the government. Although the SPLA is not the only insurgent group, it is the largest in the region.

In January 2005, the Naivasha Peace Treaty was signed between the official government of Sudan and the SPLA. This treaty essentially gave the South autonomy from the North until the end of 2010, at which time the two sides would re-examine the possibility of permanent southern independence.

The Situation in Darfur

The violence in Darfur is separate from the civil wars and the North-South conflict. The international community, including the United States, supported the Naivasha Peace Treaty and overlooked the Sudanese government's efforts to destroy the rebel groups in the South prior to its signing. But as the conflict between the North and the South appeared to be resolved, the Sudanese government escalated its assault on Darfur.

A view of Sudan's capital city, Khartoum *(at right)*.

Customarily, Darfur has been comprised of various tribal groups. Some of these groups are African in origin, while others are nomadic Arab tribes. Over the centuries, however, the people developed a common religion (Islam) and language (Arabic). The main difference between the people of Darfur is that some are herders and others are farmers. Most of the Africans are farmers and live in the more fertile southern part of Darfur. Traditionally, Arabs are herders and live closer to the Sahara Desert, the geographical border of northern Darfur and the Arab countries of North Africa. The Arabs and the Africans commonly intermarried. They also were dependent on the same land for their survival. Therefore, the distinctions between Arab and African grew smaller over the hundreds of years of Darfur's history. In fact, there are many Arabs who look more African. Similarly, many Africans are considered Arabs because of the tribes into which they have been assimilated.

Over time, the people of Darfur had established a sophisticated way of living together more or less harmoniously. Several factors disrupted this harmony. The decades of droughts destroyed most of the fertile land in the North. This forced many of the Arab herders farther and farther south. Moving their livestock to graze in the southern lands of Darfur became an issue with the southern farmers. However, because these various tribes have been living together for generations, they had a system in place to deal with these minor conflicts. More recently, the government of Khartoum has enforced laws that favor the Arab tribes over the African tribes, so it became harder for issues to be resolved locally. The harmony between the Arabs and the Africans of Darfur was destroyed by the Sudanese government and other outside forces.

Causes of the Conflict

The people of Darfur had not been involved directly in the insurgency from the South. Logically, they would be loyal to the North because they share the same religion. However, in the past few years, the government's neglect of the region's needs and the recent attacks created a new insurgency in Darfur.

The Darfur insurgency was originally called the Darfur Liberation Army (DLA). This group was comprised of members of the African Zaghawa tribes from western Darfur and Chad. With the rise in violence at the hands of the al-Bashir regime, the DLA started to see how much they had in common with the insurgents in the south of Sudan. The DLA is now called the Sudan Liberation Army (SLA), a statement that they are fighting not only for the survival of Darfur, but also for the liberation of all Sudanese affected by al-Bashir's government. The SLA began attacking police and military personnel controlled by the Sudanese government. Their most successful attack was aimed at the airport in Darfur's capital, Al-Fashir. The rebels claim that since military aircraft are used to bomb the villages, these guerrilla attacks were meant to preempt more devastation in Darfur. In response to the SLA and other newly formed rebel groups, the Sudanese army launched a counterinsurgency. Because of Darfur's inhospitable geography, however, the Sudanese army had difficulty responding to these rebels.

Therefore, the government of Khartoum enlisted nomadic Arab tribes as janjaweed to fight the rebels from within Darfur. Since the initial conflict between Arab herders and African farmers was over land rights, the nomadic Arabs were promised the land of the African tribes they defeated and destroyed. The Arab nomads launched a campaign of violence and destruction to root out the rebel groups. However, it soon became apparent that the lawlessness the government encouraged had grown out of control. The al-Bashir regime has never admitted to sponsoring this violence, even though many of the janjaweed have officially joined the Sudanese army.

There is little doubt that the janjaweed are responsible for the enormous violence perpetrated against many of the villages in Darfur. There is also little doubt that much of this activity was at the behest of the leadership in Khartoum, who saw it as a solution to their battle

A Sudan Liberation Army rebel at his base in Gellab, north Darfur.

against insurgent groups. As a result, the actions of both the Sudanese leaders and the janjaweed could be considered criminal under international law. The problem of stopping them and bringing them to justice is an extremely complex one.

Geography Is Destiny: How Darfur's Geography Affects the Current Crisis

Historians have said that geography is destiny, meaning that the natural boundaries of a place help shape the culture that develops there. Nowhere is this idea more apparent than in Darfur.

Much of the history of Sudan, the largest country in Africa, has evolved around the differences between its northern and southern regions. Darfur and the neighboring region of Kordofan comprise the western part of Sudan. Darfur has always been peripheral to the concerns of Sudan's development as a country. This fact makes the conflict in Darfur difficult to grasp because although it historically has been neglected in some ways, in other ways Darfur's geography has been crucial to Sudan's history, as both a colony and as an independent nation.

Geography of the Region

Darfur borders the countries of Chad, Libya, and the Central African Republic. The region itself, which is categorized into north and south, is approximately half the size of the country of Kenya, or equal in size to France or the state of Texas. Its vastness is one of the factors in the present conflict. Much of Darfur is not easily accessible. There are few all-weather roads, and travel in and out of the remote areas is difficult at best. The janjaweed can travel the terrain more easily than the Sudanese army; this is one of the reasons that the Sudanese government has engaged local militia to attack villagers. The remote areas limit what journalists and humanitarian workers can learn about the activity in Darfur. It is also difficult to gauge the actual number of people affected by the devastations of famine and warfare.

Darfur's Terrain

The terrain of Darfur can be categorized into four distinct parts: sand, watercourses, basement rock, and mountains. Most of the arable land in Darfur consists of goz (a soil sediment in which vegetation can grow) in the sandy region and the fertile beds of the watercourses. Goz can be useful for farming but mainly provides land for grazing herds.

The rainy season turns the watercourses, beds of land running along small bodies of water, into arable land. When the watercourses flood in the rainy season, the land surrounding them can be used to grow crops.

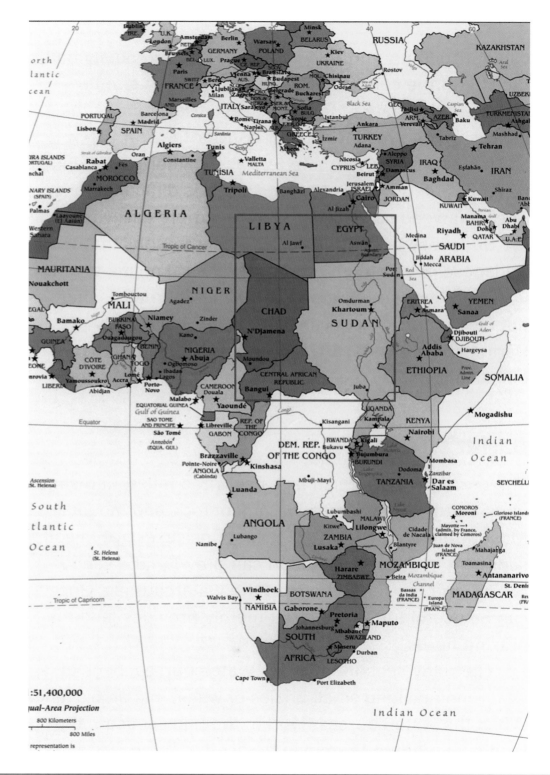

Any fertile terrain is valuable because each year a portion of the arable land decreases as the desert area increases. This process is known as desertification, and it can be a result of many factors, including drought, wind, deforestation (the cutting down of trees), overuse of land, and global environmental pollution. In Darfur, the primary cause of desertification has been the prolonged drought. However, deforestation and overuse of land are man-made causes of desertification. This has fueled the conflict between the various tribal groups, which had existed peacefully. The cycle of land erosion continues because the droughts force people to overuse the land they have, which in turn makes the land less arable and adds to desertification. This issue is also linked to global warming.

Desertification has had the most impact on the northern region of Darfur, where years may pass without rainfall. This area borders the Libyan Desert (the southern part of the Sahara Desert). In the south, where there is more abundant rainfall even during years of drought, there is little sign of land erosion. This has caused most of Darfur's population to become dependent on the arable land of the southern region. Much of the conflict

The map (at left) shows the African continent in relation to its surrounding regions. The boxed area shows Sudan and its neighbors.

in Darfur has its roots in the drought and famine that started in the 1980s. The lack of fertile land caused the populations to compete with one another for land on which they could survive.

People

The people of Darfur have a great deal in common, regardless of whether they are Arab or African, farmers or herders. The connections between them due to their shared Arabic language and Islamic faith are far greater than the differences amongst them. In recent years, outside forces have been trying to undermine the similarities between the people of Darfur and draw them into opposition with each other. The reason for this is that a divided Darfur is less of a political, economic, and military threat to the totalitarian regime in Khartoum.

Historically, the people of Darfur have had a fluid sense of identity. Because of intermarriage and migration of tribes, an individual could be African but belong to an Arab tribe, and vice versa. Sometimes tribes would intermarry in order to gain land rights. Nomadic tribes would join farming tribes in times of famine and drought. Other assimilation, or mixing, resulted from slavery.

The people of Darfur are comprised of more than seventy different tribes. The Fur tribe makes up the primary population of the region and is generally accepted

Children wait for food at a United Nations feeding center in Narsia, Sudan, in 1992. Famine in southern Sudan was caused by drought.

as indigenous, or native. (The name "Darfur" is derived from the combination of the words *dar* and *fur*, meaning "land of the Fur.") The Fur, along with the Zaghawa and the Masalit, are the main tribal groups in Darfur.

The identity of an individual person in Darfur is not predetermined by a particular ethnicity. Rather, it is connected to a person's ability to incorporate him- or herself into the customs and practices of a tribe. This is a result of the many generations of intertribal movement and assimilation.

Divisions Between the People of Darfur

The hostility between Darfur's Arabs and Africans is relatively new, but this is not to say that tribal conflict has not existed throughout the history of the region. Different groups have come into conflict over land and water rights. Fortunately, there also has been a traditional system of dealing with intertribal disputes. Elders of the conflicting tribes would reach a resolution and the members of each tribe would be bound by it. In recent years, however, al-Bashir's government has undermined tribal resolutions and has been enforcing adherence to the Sudanese legal system. Therefore, traveling courts have dealt with intertribal issues. These courts have favored the Arab tribes over the African ones because the Sudanese legal system prefers Muslims over non-Muslims. This has been another cause of the conflict between Arabs and Africans in Darfur.

The population of Sudan is approximately 40 percent Arab and 50 percent African. There is also a small Beja population (nomadic tribes living in northeastern Sudan between the Nile River and the Red Sea). The discrepancy between Arab and African populations could be a factor in the al-Bashir regime's desire to attack Darfur's African people. Genocide has historically been a means to maintain political control over another population.

Economy

The death and destruction in Darfur have a negative effect on the Sudanese economy. This fact increases the problems created by the civil war. Farming and herding drive the economy of Darfur, the population of which is approximately 15 percent of Sudan's total population. Most of Sudan's forty-one million people are engaged in farming for their livelihood. In a country that has been devastated by famine over the past three decades, every bit of food production has an enormous impact. The displacement and murder of Darfur farmers will diminish the food supply for the entire nation. The economic impact is just one of the many unforeseen circumstances of the present turmoil in Darfur.

Grains are the major staple of the Darfuris' diet. Wet-season crops such as millet, sorghum, peanuts, and sesame are their chief forms of sustenance. Sorghum is a type of cereal that grows in warm climates. It is used as a main dietary grain and also serves as feed for livestock. Millet is another cereal that can grow in poor soil. The millet seeds are used to make flour and can also be fermented to make alcohol.

Just as the cultural and ethnic differences between the people of Darfur are vague, so are the differences between farmers and herders. Many herders, for example, need to grow some crops, and many farmers need to maintain some livestock. Herders often raise a small number of different types of livestock (mainly goats, sheep, and camels). This is done to ensure the survival of their animals in case of disease (if they raised only one type of animal, a single illness could wipe them out entirely). Many herders sell their livestock to purchase grains and other materials. They are dependent on the markets and the larger economy, and are not truly nomadic.

The larger villages in Darfur typically have markets where goods and services are exchanged. There, vegetables, spices, meat, and various handmade products such as mats and baskets are sold. Firewood, an extremely important commodity, is also sold. Some people earn their livelihood by collecting firewood and selling it at the market.

Economic Aspects of the Crisis

One of the most brutal aspects of the genocide in Darfur is connected to the collection of firewood. The people who have been displaced from their villages live in refugee camps. Life in these camps depends upon the same economic forces as the world outside. Therefore, many girls work to gather firewood in the countryside surrounding the campsites. These females are most susceptible to attacks and rapes by the janjaweed and the

In western Darfur, Sudanese women carry collected firewood into a camp for internally displaced people. The wood is necessary for the survival of their families.

army. Many have been repeatedly raped. They continue this dangerous work because they need firewood and the money from its sale to survive. Men who are in the refugee camps do not collect firewood because the janjaweed or the army would kill them. Families and young children must make choices such as these: they must choose between death and rape.

Much of Darfur's economy is connected to control of the land. In fact, throughout the region's history, the economy functioned on land grants called hakuras. The sultan, or king, gave land rights to a particular family. These essentially gave the family complete control of an area of land. The land was farmed by either slave labor or hired hands. They lived on feudal estates and paid taxes to the family. Hakuras holders became both powerful and wealthy, and their land could be passed down to their heirs.

In 1916, the co-colonial government of Egypt and Great Britain outlawed the system of land grants and tried to move the economy toward herding instead of farming. However, the idea of land rights has remained a part of Darfur's culture and is deeply rooted in the people's identity. Some believe that the janjaweed are primarily motivated by the Sudanese government's promise of land grants, although there is serious doubt that the government would make or could keep such promises.

Sudan's Oil Wealth

Sudan is a very oil-rich nation. The government of Sudan, controlled by the Islamic North, has complete control of this wealth. The oil is primarily in the South, and the Chevron Oil Company only discovered it in the early

Sudan's president Omar Hassan al-Bashir *(center)* unveiled a billion-dollar oil pipeline in central Sudan, on May 31, 1999. Former president Jaafar al-Nimeri *(left, in glasses)* also attended the ceremony.

1970s. The North granted Chevron rights to drill in the South, but large-scale oil production has only begun recently. The struggle for oil wealth is one of the causes of the conflict in Sudan. Other countries, including China, India, and many European and Middle Eastern countries, would like access to this resource. As a result, numerous outside nations have invested billions of dollars in Sudan. By doing so, they are supporting the North despite the systematic killing sponsored and committed by the government both in the South and in Darfur. Thus, the Sudanese government is able to maintain control and benefit from the oil wealth.

Darfur is separated from the rest of Sudan by the region of Kordofan. The area to the east of Kordofan is in the Nile Valley. This area is far richer in resources and land.

Early civilizations in the Nile Valley were small kingdoms that depended upon the surrounding areas for food, resources, and slave labor. These surrounding areas are referred to as hinterlands (from the German word meaning "behind the land"). The power of these kingdoms came from how much of the hinterlands they could control. Areas were often raided for slaves, and many of the kingdoms protected themselves from other kingdoms with slave armies.

Tribal Culture and Islam

In the area that we know as Sudan, the influence of Islam dates back to the Middle Ages, perhaps even before the tenth century. It is believed that this Arab and Muslim influence was a result of invasions from Egypt (in the north) and from across the Red Sea (to the east). As the contact between the Nile Valley kingdoms and the Arab world increased, there was great incentive for these kingdoms' rulers to convert to Islam. Their conversion brought them greater access to trade and economic privileges and provided them with powerful allies.

The Darfur sultanate (what a kingdom was called once it converted to Islam) was established in the 1600s and had as its hinterland the region of Dar Fartit. The prominence of the Fur Sultanate is the root of much of the ethnic divisions between Africans and Arabs in Darfur today. The conversion to Islam gave the Fur sultans more power because they became a part of the Arab world. With Islam came education and more trade with other sultanates. This was the foundation of the society that later became Darfur. The Fur tribes came from the Jebel Marra Mountains and took over its surrounding areas. The people they conquered were either converted to Islam or forced to leave. Those who left became a part of the Fertit tribes. This process of assimilation formed most of the region that is present-day Darfur.

The population of the Fur Sultanate was very diverse, as it still is today. The distinction between different racial and ethic groups was less important than their connection to the sultanate. The sultans were African but culturally considered Arabs. They adapted their previous culture to their new Islamic culture. Since this was a feudal society, the people gained protection from obeying the sultan and becoming a part of that community.

Sudan's Colonial Past

The era of Darfur's independent rule ended as the result of the Turk-Egyptian invasion of North Sudan in 1820. This time period, known as the Turkiyya, occurred because Egypt and its ally Turkey were looking to expand their influence and gain resources in Africa. Much of this was influenced by the slave trade. At this time, British missionaries were also moving into Africa to convert people to Christianity. This resulted in a small Christian minority in South Sudan that exists today. The Turk-Egyptian regime eventually invaded Darfur in 1881.

A Sudanese revolt in 1885 led to the expulsion of the Turks. The Egyptians then formed an alliance with the British, known as the British-Egyptian Condominium. The two countries agreed to jointly control Sudan (although the British made all the major decisions). Many of the policies that these countries held in the years of colonization have affected the development of Sudan up to the present time.

The British achieved colonization of Sudan in stages, without a full military invasion. The slave trade and the exploitation of Sudan's resources were the main reasons for their colonization. British control of Sudan occurred during the height of European colonialism in Africa, and the British were competing against France and Belgium for control of North Africa. Darfur was valuable to the British because it served as a natural barrier against encroachment on their colony by the French.

One possible advantage of being a colony of a powerful nation is the potential for development of its infrastructure. Creating an infrastructure means that many modern necessities are built by the colonizers, including roads, railways, schools, and hospitals. Industry and agriculture are developed in order to improve the economy. The British did this to a great degree in the North and created an educated elite class of Muslims that ruled the country. Because the North was more valuable to the British, special privileges were given to the ruling Muslims, and the South was forced to submit in many ways.

The South was much less developed, despite having Christian religion in common with the British rulers. Although Darfur was of strategic importance to the British, they considered it a satellite region of the country. So they chose not to invest any resources into the development of its infrastructure. For example, by 1935 there was only one elementary school in a region as large as the state of Texas. Since Darfur has a long

In 1925, the first train passed over the Sennar Dam in Sudan, south of the capital city of Khartoum.

history as a feudal society, the British could maintain their control with little cost or effort. They basically had to make alliances with the tribal leaders.

Post-Colonialism and the Civil Wars

In February 1953, the British and the Egyptians signed an agreement providing Sudan self-governance. The South was essentially left out of this process; the official language of Sudan became Arabic. Of the hundreds of government positions vacated by the British, only a handful were given to people from the South. The climate of independent Sudan was ripe for conflict.

After Sudanese independence, Darfur could not compete politically or economically with the rest of the country. It did not have a large educated leadership and thus could not influence the political changes that were taking place in Sudan. In fact, Darfur was not even a factor in the first few decades of Sudanese independence; the real struggle during this period was between the North and the South.

Muslim military leaders in the North held the political power of the new nation. The South wanted a federal government that would give its people an equal voice. However, the forces in the North were more powerful and wanted to create an Islamic society. The South, which was mostly animist and Christian, had resources including oil, but the North still controlled the nation's wealth. These religious and economic differences erupted into the first civil war, which lasted until 1972. During this time the southern rebel groups were formed. In the North, a military leader by the name of Jaafar al-Nimeiry took control of the government. The Addis Abba Agreement (named after the capital of Ethiopia, where it was signed) ended the war. This agreement gave the South some independence and an uneasy peace that lasted for about ten years.

The Sudanese soldier at the head of the line trains anti-government rebels from the South during the first civil war in 1971.

The main opponent to Nimeiry was Sadiq al-Mahdi, a descendant of a powerful Islamic religious figure in the early movement toward Sudanese independence. The struggle between these two men defined the conflict in Sudan for the next twenty years. In addition, drought and famine increased, reaching a crisis point in 1984. The lack of food worsened the political problems of the country.

Neighboring Chad and Libya also influenced events in Darfur. These countries stood to gain control of the region by creating unrest in Sudan during the two civil wars that followed independence. The Darfuris' Muslim faith connected them to the northern government. However, the government was not doing much to help them. Therefore, the people of Darfur were more likely to join sides with the antigovernment forces in the South or with these neighboring countries.

Muammar Qaddafi and Sudan

During this time, Colonel Muammar Qaddafi, the leader of Libya, exerted great influence over the politics of Sudan, especially in Darfur. The area of Sudan had become a focal point in the Cold War between the United States and the Soviet Union. There were Communist groups in Chad and Ethiopia, countries neighboring Sudan. The United States, fearing that Libya and its ally the Soviet Union would gain control over the entire North African region, provided famine relief to Sudan. It also provided military and intelligence support through the Central Intelligence Agency (CIA). The United States hoped that supporting Sudan's government would prevent the regime in the North from falling to the Communists. (This proved to be ironic in later years since the North eventually created an Islamic government in Sudan.)

Qaddafi was interested in annexing Sudan as a part of Libya, but he failed to convince Nimeiry. In the

Colonel Muammar Qaddafi, head of the Libyan Revolutionary Council, addresses a large crowd in Libya, in 1970.

meantime, Qaddafi had created an alliance with Sadiq al-Mahdi. Qaddafi wanted to unify all of North Africa under Arab control and had a great deal of money and military power to support the Arabs in the region. Thousands of Libyan troops were sent to north Sudan to fight the South. Qaddafi's belief in Arab superiority did a great deal to create hostility between the Arabs and the Africans in Sudan, especially in Darfur. Libya had stationed troops in Darfur to help the Arabs in Chad, who were also in the midst of a civil war. Since the

United States was enemies with Qaddafi, and Qaddafi was supported by the Soviet Union, this created an influx of weapons into Sudan from all sides. In fact, some of these Soviet-era airplanes, called Antanovs, are used today to destroy the villages in Darfur.

In 1985, Nimeiry was overthrown in a coup, and in 1986, Sadiq al-Mahdi was elected but did not stay in power. By 1989, al-Bashir had taken control of Sudan in a military coup. Al-Bashir's government is a fundamentalist regime, and his main focus has been to make the government of Sudan Islamic.

Sudan's Recent Past

Much of what is happening in Darfur has occurred throughout world history. Similar events have also developed in other parts of Sudan in recent years. In the 1980s, the Dinka tribe suffered a fate comparable to what is currently taking place in Darfur. The Dinka lived in a region of southern Sudan known as Bahar al-Ghazal. During a civil war, Arab militias called the Muraheleen attacked many Dinka villages. These raids were meant to destroy rebel strongholds in the south of Sudan. As a result, thousands of Dinka were killed and thousands more were displaced. Many of them fled to the southern region of Darfur. Some are still there and are experiencing this fate a second time.

Even after a peace agreement ended the second civil war between North and South, the impact of the death and destruction has continued. It is virtually impossible for the refugees to return to their homes, many of which have been destroyed. A larger obstacle is that the infrastructure—the roads, power lines, and additional structures needed for society to function—is no longer there. The two civil wars had a tremendously negative impact on the long-term economic potential of Sudan. These patterns are being repeated again in Darfur. The massive number of Darfuri refugees who are fleeing to Chad has adversely affected Chad and is driving it toward a war with the government of Sudan.

Osama bin Laden's Ties to Sudan

Osama bin Laden lived in Khartoum in the 1980s, and in the 1990s, he and his Al Qaeda terrorist network functioned out of Sudan. On August 20, 1998, under President Bill Clinton, the U.S. military bombed a pharmaceutical factory in Shifa, Sudan. This was in retaliation for the Al Qaeda bombings of the U.S. embassies in Kenya and Tanzania earlier that month, which killed more than 250 people and injured more than 4,000. It was believed that bin Laden financed the Shifa factory to manufacture chemical weapons to be used in other attacks.

At a meeting in August 2005, Omar Hassan al-Bashir *(center, facing camera)* greets Salva Kiir, leader of the Sudan People's Liberation Army.

After the September 11, 2001, Al Qaeda attacks on New York City and Washington, D.C., President George W. Bush supported al-Bashir's Sudanese regime in the hopes that it would help the United States in its efforts against bin Laden. (Bin Laden left Sudan for Afghanistan in 1996 and is believed to have been in Pakistan around the time of the 9/11 attacks.) The willingness of the Khartoum regime under al-Bashir to help the United States caused the Bush administration to see it as an ally against terrorism. The United States, hoping to maintain this relationship, forced the compromise between Khartoum and the Sudan People's Liberation Army (SPLA) in 2005. Some people believe that U.S. pressure for a peace agreement caused the violence in Darfur to be overlooked. However, the world would soon discover that al-Bashir had begun massive attacks against the people of Darfur even while negotiating peace with the SPLA in the South.

What Is Genocide?

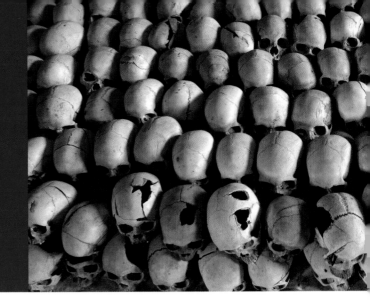

The violence in Darfur has been referred to as genocide. This word has deep consequences in terms of the response of the international community.

Genocide vs. Ethnic Cleansing

Both genocide and ethnic cleansing refer to the large-scale killing of a specific portion of a population of people. The difference between the two terms is the extent and intention of the group doing the killing. Genocide is meant to destroy a group of people completely, while ethnic cleansing is meant to weaken and remove the survivors from the country. In either case, the impact on the population being attacked is enormous. Those who survive and their future generations will feel the effects of this suffering. There have been many examples of genocide in the past century: the genocide of Armenians by the Ottoman Turks in 1915; the Nazis' genocide of Jews during World War II; the

Cambodian genocide by the Khmer Rouge in the 1970s; and the genocide in Rwanda, Sudan's African neighbor, in the 1990s.

Although the government of Sudan refuses to admit that it is trying to systematically kill the African population of Darfur, there is little doubt that it is doing so. The reason there is any debate by the international community has a lot to do with the United Nations (UN) and its standards for human rights. In 1948, after the end of World War II, the International Convention on the Prevention and Punishment of Crimes of Genocide was held to discuss issues of human rights. On December 10, 1948, the General Assembly of the UN established the Universal Declaration of Human Rights, which has served as an international constitution of human rights. Genocide is considered an international crime.

The Rome Statute and the International Criminal Court

The Rome Statute, an agreement of 120 nations to be subject to international laws regarding human rights, established the International Criminal Court (ICC) in 2000. Any violation of these laws could result in ICC prosecution of government leaders. Seven countries, including the United States, have refused to sign the Rome Statute and subject themselves to prosecution for

Sudan president Omar Hassan al-Bashir shakes hands with U.S. Secretary of State Colin Powell *(left)* in Khartoum on June 29, 2004. Powell's visit focused on humanitarian relief for the crisis in Darfur.

human rights violations and war crimes. In fact, President George W. Bush signed the American Service-Members' Protection Act, which says the United States will use military force to protect any Americans from prosecution by the ICC.

During the first few years of the conflict in Darfur, the UN did not label the violence as genocide. Some international leaders, including the U.S. secretary of state at the time, Colin Powell, disagreed. To this day, the debate continues because the government of Sudan insists that the violence in Darfur is a result of local tribal tensions and their attempts to respond to a rebellion. As long as the international community does not agree that the killing is genocide, it remains an internal matter for the government of Sudan, and its leaders are not subject to prosecution by the ICC.

The Role of the International Community

In addition to the United Nations, the African Union (AU) has had a large role in trying to stop the violence in Darfur. Originally called the Organization of African Unity, the AU is an organization of fifty-two African nations that was formed in 2000. (It became known as the AU in 2002.) It is similar to the European Union (EU) in that its purpose is to promote the peace, cooperation, security, and economic development of its member nations. The conflict in Darfur has been the first real test for this organization. In the period following the signing of the Naivasha Peace Treaty and as international attention was drawn to the region, Sudan's government refused to allow UN peacekeeping troops into Darfur, but it allowed a small number of AU troops. Despite these efforts, the killing in Darfur has continued.

In October 2006, the UN envoy to Sudan, Jan Pronk, criticized al-Bashir's government and said it was responsible for the killing in Darfur. The Sudanese government

In June 2006, an African Union (AU) soldier patrols a camp for the internally displaced just south of El Fasher, in the western part of Darfur.

called these statements outrageous and expelled Pronk from Sudan. Despite this occurrence, Kofi Annan, the secretary general of the UN—whose term ended at the conclusion of 2006—continued to negotiate with the Sudanese government. In November 2006, they reached an agreement to allow UN peacekeeping forces into Darfur. The agreement will provide more money and support for AU troops. This was generally seen as progress toward peace in Darfur, although the outcome of this agreement still remains to be seen.

The Role of Darfur Within Sudan

There is a general fear by the government of Khartoum that the peace agreement with the SPLA will not work out—after all, they have been warring since the 1950s. If the non-Muslim African South allies itself with the Africans in Darfur, they could create a real opposition to the Khartoum regime. The Africans in Darfur are Muslims, but they have much more in common with the South than the North. During the civil wars, many Darfuris were drafted by the North to fight in the South. These drafts were very unpopular, proof that there is a tendency in Darfur to side with the South. Al-Bashir's regime has done everything it can to destroy the people of Darfur before they can become a threat. The North-South peace agreement actually has contributed to the genocide in Darfur because the Khartoum government is trying to maintain as much control over all of Sudan as it possibly can.

Why Darfur Matters to the Rest of the World

artin Luther King Jr. once said, "Injustice anywhere is a threat to justice everywhere." If we can understand what this means, then we can understand why the suffering of others should concern us.

We Are All Affected

The current situation in Darfur affects all of us indirectly. As the earth's population increases, the global economy expands and natural resources dwindle. People of all nations become more dependent upon one another for their means of support.

Human beings have more in common with one another than almost any other species on the planet. When scientists mapped the human genome in 2001, they discovered that all humans are 99.9 percent identical on a genetic level. That means the measurable difference between any two people on the planet is one-tenth of 1 percent. In other words, the differences of race, religion, nationality, and gender are small when compared to the vast similarities between all human beings.

Much of the violence in Africa is a result of the dictatorial rulers misusing their power. Despite abusing and exploiting their population, these rulers have the vast wealth of the region in their hands, so international businesses and governments continue to deal with them. As long as these policies continue, the violence will continue.

The sovereign governments of Africa, especially Sudan, have claimed that the entrance of UN troops and international peacekeepers is another form of colonialism. In the recent past, they used this argument to resist the presence of the United Nations. The former head of the United Nations, Kofi Annan, and others have denied these accusations. In addition, many feel that the international community has a responsibility to help those in Darfur. They feel that the Sudanese government has been making excuses to prevent outside aid to the people of Darfur.

The Impact of the International Community

In the summer and late fall of 2006, major changes were made to how the international community would respond to the situation in Darfur. In August, the UN Security Council passed a resolution to send peacekeeping troops to protect civilians in Darfur. The Sudanese government resisted this move until the late fall, when it agreed to allow the international troops into the region.

Despite the appearance of progress, the violence in Darfur has reached a critical point, also creating violence in Chad. Many rebel groups have been attempting to organize and recruit across the border in Chad. The janjaweed pursued these rebels and attacked the villagers living near the border, thus continuing the violence into the neighboring country. The presence of the United Nations and African Union troops has not stopped this bloodshed. In fact, the rampant violence has created more violence. The lawlessness of the region has created an environment where the people are not even safe from the forces sent there to help them: several dozen UN soldiers have been under investigation for sexual abuse of girls in Darfur.

Kofi Annan has said that the crisis in Darfur is the result of a global failure. In his final speech as secretary general of the UN on December 11, 2006, he stated the five lessons he leaves those who will now deal with these critical issues:

> *First, we are all responsible for each other's security. Second, we can and must give everyone the chance to benefit from global prosperity. Third, both security and prosperity depend on human rights and the rule of law. Fourth, states*

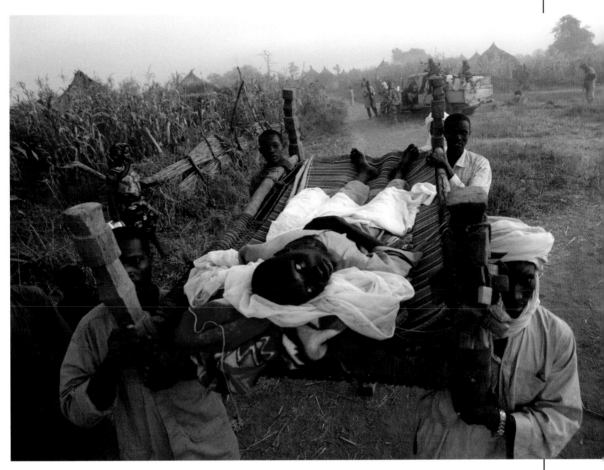

The violence in Darfur has spread to regions in neighboring Chad. On November 13, 2006, Chadian villagers rescue a wounded man.

must be accountable to each other, and to a broad range of non-state actors, in their international conduct. My fifth and final lesson derives inescapably from those other four. We can only do all these things by working together.

Annan's words are much like Martin Luther King's: the responsibility for peace and justice in the world begins with each individual.

What the Future Holds

The international community is pressing the United Nations' new secretary general, Ban Ki-moon, to make the Darfur region a top priority. It is hoped that he will support the resolutions passed under Kofi Annan and ensure that the United Nations and the African Union continue to address the violence in the region. However, it is still unclear whether the resolutions adopted by the UN will be effective.

On December 14, 2006, outgoing United Nations Secretary General Kofi Annan *(left)* shakes hands with his successor, Ban Ki-moon *(right)*.

Glossary

Addis Abba Agreement The 1972 North-South treaty that ended Sudan's first civil war.

African Union (AU) Formerly called the Organization of African Unity; the organization of fifty-two nations designed to promote the peace, cooperation, security, and economic development of its member nations.

animist A religious belief in a supernatural power that organizes the universe.

annex To take possession or conquer; occupy.

arable Farmable, fertile land; suitable for growing crops.

assimilate To take in, absorb, and integrate people, ideas, or culture into a wider society or culture.

asylum A place of refuge and protection.

behest An order or command.

catalyst A spark, or stimulation, for another event.

Cold War A state of conflict between two countries without direct military combat, especially the hostility between the United States and the Soviet Union from 1945 to 1990.

colonialism The policy of taking control of another country in order to gain an economic advantage.

Communist A follower of Communism, a political theory that supports a society where all property is publicly owned and every person is paid according to his or her abilities and needs.

counterinsurgency Military or political action taken against the activities of guerrillas or revolutionaries.

coup A military overthrow of a government.

Darfur Liberation Army (DLA) A Darfur-based insurgency group that later became the Sudan Liberation Army.

divisive Tending to cause a disagreement or hostility between groups or persons.

encroachment The act of entering gradually or stealthily, often taking away authority, rights, or property of another.

envoy A representative on a diplomatic mission.

fundamentalist Strict maintenance of ancient doctrines of any religion or ideology, notably Islam. Also used to refer to a form of Protestant Christianity following literal interpretations of the Bible.

goz Sandy soil that becomes fertile land with small amounts of rainfall.

guerrilla A member of a small independent group taking part in irregular fighting against an organized military force.

hakuras Traditional tribal land rights given to a person by the leader of the tribe.

hinterland A German word meaning "behind the land." It refers to the area surrounding the center of a kingdom from which resources and people are obtained.

innate Inborn or natural (as opposed to being acquired).

insurgency A rising or active revolt.

International Criminal Court (ICC) The international court responsible for trying those accused of war crimes, genocide, and crimes against humanity. The ICC does not replace national courts. Instead, it works with national criminal court systems. The ICC is located in the Hague, Netherlands.

Islam The religion of Muslims; a faith with one God revealed through Muhammad as the prophet of Allah.

janjaweed An Arab militia backed by the government of Sudan that has been attacking African villages in Darfur.

Mahdi In Muslim belief, a divine prophet with super-natural powers.

Naivasha Peace Treaty The peace accord reached by the government of Sudan with insurgency groups in the South, primarily the SPLA, which allows for the independence of the South in several stages. This treaty was signed in 2005.

nomadic Traveling from place to place, with no permanent abode.

perpetrate To carry out or commit a harmful, illegal, or immoral action.

regime A particular government, especially one considered to be oppressive.

Rome Statute The international agreement of 120 nations to hold themselves and other nations accountable for war crimes and crimes against humanity under the jurisdiction of the ICC.

sovereign The supreme ruler of a monarchy.

Sudan Liberation Army (SLA) The main insurgency militia in Darfur, formerly called the Darfur Liberation Army.

Sudan People's Liberation Army (SPLA) The main insurgency militia in South Sudan that opposed the government of Sudan in the North. The SPLA signed the Naivasha Peace Treaty in 2005.

sultanate A Muslim sovereign ruler.

totalitarian A one-party dictatorship.

watercourse A bed along which flows a stream, brook, or artificially constructed channel of water.

For More Information

African Union Headquarters
P.O. Box 3243
Addis Ababa
Ethiopia
Web site: http://www.africa-union.org

Office for the Coordination of Humanitarian
    Affairs (OCHA)
United Nations Secretariat, S-3600
New York, NY 10017
(212) 963-1234
Web site: http://ochaonline.un.org

Royal African Society (RAS)
c/o School of Oriental and African Studies
Thornhaugh Street, Russell Square
London, WC1H 0XG
United Kingdom
Web site: http://www.royalafricansociety.org

UNICEF (United Nations International Children's
    Emergency Fund)
National Headquarters
333 East 38th Street

New York, NY 10016

(212) 686-5522

Web site: http://www.unicefusa.org

United States Agency for International
       Development (USAID)
Information Center, Ronald Reagan Building
Washington, DC 20523-1000
(202) 712-4810
Web site: http://www.usaid.gov

Web Sites

Due to the changing nature of Internet links, Rosen
Publishing has developed an online list of Web sites
related to the subject of this book. This site is updated
regularly. Please use this link to access the list:

http://www.rosenlinks.com/itn/daag

For Further Reading

Burr, J. Millard, and Robert O. Collins. *Darfur: The Long Road to Disaster*. Princeton, NJ: Markus Weiner Publishers, 2006.

DiPiazza, Francesca Davis. *Sudan in Pictures* (Visual Geography Series). Minneapolis, MN: Twenty-First Century Books, 2006.

Fisanick, Christina. *Genocide* (Opposing Viewpoints). Farmington Hills, MI: Greenhaven Press, 2007.

Flint, Julie, and Alex de Waal. *Darfur: A Short History of a Long War* (African Arguments). London, England: Zed Books, 2006.

January, Brendan. *Genocide: Modern Crimes Against Humanity*. Minneapolis, MN: Twenty-First Century Books, 2007.

Marlowe, Jen, Aisha Bain, and Adam Shapiro. *Darfur Diaries: Stories of Survival*. New York, NY: Nation Books, 2006.

Montgomery, Lane H. *Never Again, Again, Again... Genocide: Armenia to Darfur*. New York, NY: Ruder Finn Press, 2007.

Naidoo, Beverly, ed. *Making It Home: Real-Life Stories from Children Forced to Flee*. New York, NY: Dial Books for Young Readers, 2005.

Sheehan, Sean. *Genocide* (Face the Facts). Chicago, IL: Raintree Publishing, 2005.

Spangenburg, Ray, and Kit Moser. *The Crime of Genocide: Terror Against Humanity* (Issues in Focus). Berkeley Heights, NJ: Enslow Publishers, 2000.

Springer, Jane. *Genocide* (Groundwork Guides). Toronto, ON: Groundwood Books, 2006.

Totten, Samuel, and Eric Markusen, eds. *Genocide in Darfur: Investigating the Atrocities in the Sudan.* New York, NY: Routledge Books, 2006.

Bibliography

Anderson, Scott. "How Did Darfur Happen?" *New York Times*. October 17, 2004.

Annan, Kofi. *Address at Truman Presidential Museum and Library*, Independence, MO. December 11, 2006.

De Waal, Alex. *Famine That Kills: Darfur, Sudan.* Revised ed. New York, NY: Oxford University Press, 2005.

Gettleman, Jeffrey. "War in Sudan? Not Where the Oil Wealth Flows." *New York Times*. October 24, 2006.

Johnson, Douglas H. *The Root Causes of Sudan's Civil Wars* (African Issues). Bloomington, IN: Indiana University Press, 2003.

Kahn, Joseph. "China Courts Africa, Angling for Strategic Gains." *New York Times*. November 3, 2006.

Kristof, Nicholas D. "The Face of Genocide." *New York Times*. November 19, 2006.

Kristof, Nicholas D. "Genocide in Slow Motion." (Review of *Darfur: A Short History of a Long War* and *Darfur: The Ambiguous Genocide*.) *New York Review of Books*. February 9, 2006.

Kristof, Nicholas D. "A Sister's Sacrifice." *New York Times*. November 26, 2006.

Kristof, Nicholas D. "Why Genocide Matters." *New York Times*. September 10, 2006.

Polgreen, Lydia. "The World; Rwanda's Shadow, from Darfur to Congo." *New York Times*. July 23, 2006

Prunier, Gérard. *Darfur: The Ambiguous Genocide.* Ithaca, NY: Cornell University Press, 2005.

Rubin, Elizabeth. "If Not Peace, Then Justice." *New York Times*. April 2, 2006.

Schneider, Daniel B. "UN to Limit the Role of Its Envoy Expelled by Sudan." *New York Times*. October 28, 2006.

Sengupta, Somini. "Crisis in Sudan: Thorny Issues Underlying Carnage in Darfur Complicate World's Response." *New York Times*. August 16, 2004.

Shapiro, Adam, director. *Darfur Diaries: Message from Home.* 2005. DVD. Cinema Libre Studio, 2006.

Traub, James. "China's African Adventure." *New York Times*. November 19, 2006.

Worth, Robert F. "Sudan Says It Will Accept UN-African Peace Force in Darfur." *New York Times*. November 17, 2006.

Index

About the Author

John Xavier holds a Master's of Fine Arts degree in writing from Columbia University. He is a high school English teacher in Brooklyn, New York, where he resides with his wife, daughter, and dog.

Photo Credits